CSU Poetry Series LXVI

Cleveland State University Poetry Center

Hunger Wide as Heaven

poems by Max Garland

Hunger Wide as Heaven

Acknowledgments

I am grateful to the editors of the following publications in which some of these poems first appeared:

Arts and Letters: "The Pigs Hold Up the Dawn," "Goldfinches."
Crazy Horse: "The Linden in Winter," "What About the Linden."
Cream City Review: "Bible Days."
Dogwood: "For No Man Would Say He Did a Favor to the Fountain by Drinking, or to the Light by Seeing," "King of the Lilies."
Georgia Review: "You Miss It."
Gettysburg Review: "What About the Light on the Window," "Scene from a Window Near the Austin Airport," "Day So Bright," "An Exercise in Waking Up On Davenport Street."
Maize: "Oxygen," "Springfield."
New England Review: "Apparition."
Poetry: "A Night at St. Mary's."
Prairie Schooner: "The Day Lilies," "The Loon," "Child Christmas," "The Catalpa," "Christmas Concert," "Early Work," "For Who Shall Inherit."
Sycamore Review: "Homer."

Additionally, several poems in this manuscript appeared in the chapbook *Apparition* (Parallel Press).

I'd also like to thank the Wisconsin Arts Board, the Bush Foundation, and the University of Wisconsin-Eau Claire for their generous support. Thanks to Susan Grimm at CSUPC for her valuable editorial assistance.

Published by Cleveland State University Poetry Center
Department of English
2121 Euclid Avenue
Cleveland, OH 44115-2214

ISBN: 1-880834-69-3

Library of Congress Catalog
Card Number: 2005932958

Ohio Arts Council

A STATE AGENCY THAT SUPPORTS
PUBLIC PROGRAMS
IN THE ARTS
40 Years

Contents

for my sister, Pam

I

I Drift Off During the Waning Moments of Methodism

In the beginning it was Sunday
and church everlasting
as if God carved the oak pews stiff
to save the mortal soul
from softness, yet

varnished them slick
to ease the slide
should I fall asleep
and down through the smoky
scuffs and patterns
of the devil's linoleum.

Or maybe I'm just distracted
unto drowsiness
by the Bible falling
word by word
like a fine lace of Elizabethan rain
on the tawdriness of my attention
in the waning moments of Methodism,

or maybe it's just boyhood's end
God watches through the windows.
There's a red shard of stained glass
he seems to favor, so we all appear
to be burning. Though at other times

God unveils himself in the pulses
of my mother's perfume,
so close and faintly drumming,
and then it's no longer Sunday,
and I don't know what to worship,

though a flower comes to mind
that I would like to marry.

Early Work

My father's milk truck bounces
the county roads, as much a part
of the jangle of future as dawn.

His shirt is white as God to me.
I get to ride along sometimes.
The smell of the cooler

is the rubbery cold where
nothing spoils, where rows
of bottles ride like music

before the choir wakes up,
or the pigeons tear loose
from silos and steeples.

The cords of muscle in his arms,
the pulsing star of cigarette,
the jump on the waking world we get

as we navigate the deep blue
stutter of washboard roads,
help lift the day onto the calendar.

First light arrives, slow as a wage
I don't yet know the meaning of, though
I feel the glow of usefulness

as I lug the empties back to the truck
where the sun has started
to brighten the fenders and latches,

the chrome of the hubcaps like coins
for the road where dark is spent
and wealth is milk at every door.

Homer

The dark goes haywire, streaks
of underlit clouds everywhere in the east.
It's a dull town, but morning doesn't mind,
the sun still barely tucked in the pocket
of pre-dawn—and these long lit clouds?
Homer, who was blind, called them rose-fingered.
To me they're that corny shade of pink
Vasari used to paint the heavens of the holy rich.
On the other hand, light *as a hand*
is what Homer implied,
that the day reaches
up into the dark, a finger at a time,
though he couldn't have seen it—
the stroke of early light across the face,
the bark of the gull ignited—
he was right about that, and the rose
was how warm it felt to be that right.
All poets are blind to the world
without imagining, might be the point.
It's physical, this daybreak, long
lit clouds over the cold town.
Dawn in the fingers duly writing this down.
It's so small, that first breach of warm
on the window, the skin. Finger of dawn,
and therefore a hand, and therefore
a body, and therefore a mind
whose illumined reach is day
that put out Homer's eye,
that light might rake the low ledges
of cloud and gull wing and grace
the dull town breaking alive.

Motorola

My father wedged the TV sideways
through the narrow trailer door.

It took time to come alive—

a primal buzz
like something potent
barely under wraps,
a gathering of unseen agitations,
then the pinpoint of light
like a star down a well,
and the image rippling outward,
black and white, shades
of staticky gray.

You had to sink the antenna
deep, rush out in the wind
and turn it by hand,
the leafless
aluminum branches
sorting space
for the right waves—

the ones engraved with the bloodless
murder cracked in the nick of time,

the waves of cued laughter—
George Burns and baby-
voiced Gracie, whose literal mind
was the running joke.

All George had to do was pause,
kiss the tip of his cigar, smoke
catching the klieg lights, and
let language work against her.

Though in the beginning it didn't work
quite well enough to ruin our lives.

Some nights every character
trailed a pack of ghosts. Pale
trinities of gunfighters
strode the electrons to their deaths
amid blizzards and choirs
of trespassing voices. You had to
fly it like an airplane, keep things
horizontal, keep the ground
on the ground, for instance,
and always the void from infringing.

And it's not like we sparkled so much
to begin with, not like we weren't
already acquainted with ruin.

Cursed is the ground for thy sake
the Bible said the Lord said,
in sorrow shalt thou eat of it
all the days...

And sure enough
the ragweed flourished,
the pale pink heads of thistles
nodded above the fields
back of the beat down fence,

and we knew blown dust
was the one sure blossom
always willing to return.

It bloomed like a promise
against the louvered windows,

whether we rolled them out or in.

And didn't the set just sell us back
a coveting we already owned?
But this time with banter
and cleavage so lush
handkerchiefs could be tucked within,
rolls of twenties, small revolvers.

There is no record of this, no study
of how frail and jittery the hours grew,
all those evenings of discounted moonlight.
how we laughed the paneling
half apart, and wanted our way

past the beanfields and river
into the bosom of *happening,*
the faint blue source itself,
and the music thereof, bright
smoke and gunshot,
until we could no longer see
what didn't flicker,

until what we needed were *lines,*
we thought, instead of the little
we knew how to say. What we needed
were stories to be, lives
that cut to the chase, instead
of horizons of heat-warped air,
and the dull props our bodies were.

The Day Lilies

Whole bees dart into the lilies,
but the day is a blossom too.
The lilies are huge yellow hybrids,
mostly. The bees are drowning in luck.
I wonder if it even seems like work
bounding from anther to anther.
I wonder if there's a wake
of pollen in the air, a thin
gold script to the hive
I can't see? A low wind
navigates the leaves and slick stalks
of the lilies. Six petals apiece
flail outward, mouthlike and deep.

And either it's just me,
or there's something in the flowers,
the stamina shot forth
bright as flares, the yellow petals
ascending to pink, backbending
and rippling out paper thin,
almost maroon at the edges,
that looks like astonishment
scorched halfway to anger,
as if even the lilies can't believe,
given winter in the bulb, the weight
and burn of ice, the long
blind watery climb to light,
a day is all they get.

King of the Lilies

I'm considering the lilies again
as Jesus recommended back in 1959
from the pages of my grandmother's Bible.
Jesus spoke in blood, a beautiful English.
Why take ye thought for raiment?
Jesus was a regular king of the lilies.
When I consider them again, and
I'm thinking of the day lilies now,
jagged and bright as blown apart kisses,
I'm amazed at the slippery back-dive
of petals, and how quietly the pollen
blazes away, like the fall
of a tiny unspeakable language.
I think the point of the scripture was faith,
as least in my grandmother's reading.
She prayed so long and hard for so little,
the wake of her going still sounds
like the riffling of hymnbooks and Bibles.
Or maybe the point was simply
God provides, infuses, aspiring
always toward some blossom
of pure poise. Or maybe
the point was still forming
in Jesus' mind as he spoke.
Maybe even doubt is a little divine.
He'd just come from the wilderness,
after all. He knew his life was a day
nearly done. He knew the people
were ragged, love-scarred. Would despair
be a better flower? I'd believe in a Jesus
who considered that, Grandmother,
as he looked at the fields of lilies afloat.

Springfield

The days break their backs on the wide brown water.
You can see the warped spine of the river
between the girders of the Brookport Bridge.
Blue-gray stitch of a heron. Gull flight below
and the scar of its shadow on the current.

Once we've crossed the Ohio, it's the *North,*
the word bearing the lisp of disapproval.

Over the radio announcers' pitch, slick as glitter,
my father's fury lasts for miles
at what some people charge for a gallon of gas.

The more the Baptist steeples thin,
the more the horizon smells like money.

By the outskirts of Springfield,
whatever we say makes the waitresses smile.
I begin to notice my mother's voice
is like a hat with too many feathers for here.

My own becomes a kind of mumble.
Tell the lady what you want, my father says,
but even he knows, as he feels for his wallet,
we're no longer on the map.

Bible Days

God was the knife my grandfather used
to slit the belly of the fish, scrape
and finger the insides out.

God was the nail in the palm,
sword in side, splintered light
on morning grass.

When my uncle rose
and burst into tongues,
God was the syllable he sought.

You had to ransack speech
for God. You had to lose good sense
like Jonah, or Job.

When the preacher eased my parents under
and they sprang up wet and shining,
like human fish, or full grown babies,

I knew God was their father and mother
and fate, and I
was the fish out of water then.

Lilies lined the altar rail.
Mary was the rose of the windows,
always. But God was the thorn

that had to pierce the heart
before it flowered, the wound
I sat and waited for

as the choir trailed away
and the preacher found the page
where our days all turn to dust.

Chronicle

There were days when each child born
was lord of something older than time,
nights when any star you looked beneath
was hiding a baby god—

red-faced, bawling as only the young
and holy can.

There were days when the dead rose
and nights when the live descended
so deep within themselves
it was best to let them go.

There were stretches of evening
made of paper and shadow.

You were no richer for having lived them,
nor were they subtracted from the span of a life.

Because it seemed important and beyond us,
sometimes we wrote things down
with what technique we had—

vowels for the wind, consonants
for the wind to lean upon and bow.

Dear Lord

The heat bears down, steals the starch from the catalpa leaves.
They hang like outlived wishes, like their hearts, big as wind,
clean as uncut clover, are on the brink of being drained of wonder
by the lack of rain. What's a leaf to do? What's a man?
The light pokes along like a stick between the bars of the cage
of a large bored animal. But how bored, really?

By noon the sun knows things we thought were drowned
deep in the morning shadows. By four or five or some
melted hour, the county road softens and gives off the unrequited
odor of swamp. The heat is as much of the body as blood.
There's something faintly Biblical in the incantations
of the only cicada with spunk enough to sing.

If a cloud sailed by we'd salute him like an angel. If an angel
blundered down we'd have to bind his wings with baling wire,
Dear Lord, and hold him till the rains came.

Dry Spell

You could smell the river in your sleep
or what had been the river
in what would have been sleep
if the blades of the window fan
could inflict the air
with will enough to stir.

The bedsheets stuck like stamps,
but you were not delivered.

Nor was the owl calling
from the dry mouth of the barn
much help, nor were the June bugs
ratcheting up the ripped screen.

Nor were your sins that easy
not to count, as the hall clock
ticked like God's cane tapping,
like He had all night to find you,
and could make a thousand more
from the same general dust,
just as long and breathless.

And somewhere in the distance
either a coal train coupled hard,
or a drunk died at the wheel,
or maybe thunder
was learning to growl.

And the thought of that,
once you added thirst,
was like a Bible the size
of the night cracked apart,
and you didn't care
what flood came later,
as long as the rain came now.

For a Storm Along Highway 305

The doors to the shadows
were quick as winks to open.
Rain in the hinges, backwaters
of rust limbered up, let go.

Every storm or so the barn
fell dark as the will
of a bent nail. From the bitten
sides of the feed trough
every grievance welled up to air.

I remember the flicker before wind
struck the light switch blind.
The stamping of hooves in a stall.
A warped board flapped and yearned
as the weather vane spun

like the souls of the lost
when the preacher knocked
like thunder on their brows,
and we all knew so deep a drought
could only end in flood.

A Brief Religious History of Bedtime

I believed God was up the chimney
reading our minds like magazines
in barber shops. I mean, whatever there is
beyond space and time, you know
there's a lot of it to kill. I tried praying
past the pages I wanted God to miss.

Every star above the fescue field
was a promise I'd surely broken.
A mother's heart was glass like that.
A lie was a wrist-thick twist
in the soul grown over.

The best bet was your worst sin
got lost in the rush hours of God's attention,
maybe as he counted the feathers
of sparrows' wings as they bathed in dust,
or measured the might of the hairs
in the mane of the plow horse,

or answered the appeals of the angels
I sometimes swore I saw
gliding up and down the light shafts
when the summer storm was over
and the catalpa leaves held the world
rounded into water beads
you could shake loose like God
if you wanted.

Which was a sin, of course, to think
yourself above the world,
like Adam, like Eve,
like any apple you wanted was yours—

of his eye, of his knowing,
of your own mind sealed
beyond time or detection,
the unreadably sweet within.

The Catalpa

—for my sister

The day the sow nearly trotted us down,
treed us, in fact,
the world was glitter and dross.
Television was still young, like us—
like us, was full of elsewhere.
The Russians were written
into the Book of Revelations.
Riding nightmares would they come
with ash marks on their foreheads.
Thank God the fields were Christian
then. Jesus was our rabbit's foot.
Jesus was the meadowlark
who sang how the rich would moan
and rue the day, and the meek
inherit the way the sun
gilded the river and tin roof
of the trailer. Meanwhile,
although we teased her only
a little, the sow lifted herself
from the wallow, shook flecks
of gray mud away, began to move,
a kind of quaking canter, wobbly
as a planet, heavy as a planet,
but faster than we believed,
hooves quick as butcher knives,
and the low fork of the catalpa,
budded, almost in bloom,
is all that saved us, Sister,
from knowing something
else about meat
besides the sizzle and smell
as we opened the trailer door
and sat us down to thank
the Lord, our flesh
still on our bones,
our hunger wide as heaven.

It Was All Supposed to be Holy and Magnificent

They plump you up and toddle you out.
It's your oyster, the wide world is—
the paragon of animals, beauty of the lily.
Just listen how the language threads the air.
It's amazing what they've woven from nothing.
You'd think this life a living garment.
You, with your own name now,
that beads and rolls and waits
to be spoken, then quivers
like a raindrop at the end of a leaf.

The Pigs Hold Up the Dawn

—Los cerdos sostienen la aurora.
                    —Pablo Neruda

When I had grace and beauty
and four fine hooves, better than a devil's,
quite frankly, the way things tapered to a point
was not unlike the flamenco's sudden strike
of heel on barren ground. And did I not run like driving rain
after long drought to the trough, and did I not feed
shoulder to shoulder with the greater and lesser
of my kind, as if the spell of hunger made us
sister and brother. And when the day grew warm
and red, and when the scent of the world rose
and gave the brain direction and will enough
to move this bulk, my body, from barn to wallow,
from ruined field to shadow of cedars, was I not
among the pillars of diligence and mirth
that helped the sun that grazed the world,
and each morning in goodness grew.

Oxygen

If songs live in the radio next to bad weather warnings
and the price of hogs, and the dial can let them out,
like opening a safe, why am I stuck here
with a nine-year-old heart, planted
upon the small skeleton I can feel
sometimes when I sleep wrong?

How do you find the true size of yourself
when God is back in the Bible, still toting
the animals up and teaching the Israelites
where not to look?

Sometimes I feel the heat of what Elvis means
when his voice stutters like a rusted muffler
and I think the radio is God of this house,
and the commandments are tucked
into the elements of my body
I'm just learning the names of in school
and how they make you up
like a story, or a song.

But who will let you out, like real music,
I wonder, like the hand on the dial of the radio,
let you be the size of the world you hear,
when God's busy back in the *shall not*s
and burning shrubs, and no one else is in the room?

Instructions and Admonitions

If it burns, don't touch it.
If it's bleach, don't taste.

If it's a bell, come home
or school's out

or the Lord's Day is upon us,
the spirit collecting itself

from the matted fleece of clouds
and the intricate branches

to fill up the church like breath
in a balloon.

If it rains, seek shelter.
Swim with a buddy.

Consider the lilies.

If it hurts, that's life.
If it bleeds, apply pressure.

Elevate the wound.
Don't panic.

If it's the world,
bless your heart,

it's not your home.

Child Christmas

I wanted god in a manger.
This was Christmas in Kentucky—1960?61?
There were flurries in the forecast.
You could fluff him up, the god
I wanted. Stacked beneath
the aluminum tree
were gifts you could depend upon.
I was ten, eleven. I wanted god
the wise child, not god
the father, not god
the bad red fist of judgment.
They had vaporized an island,
the atoms had, to save us all.
I wanted god the snowflake,
shy lamb, spankless star
atop the tree.

At school we crouched to dodge the blast
that never came, but could.
Small birds were god's to mind,
and cattle knelt for him.

I watched the sky all morning,
for snow was hallelujah
escaped from hymns to shower us.

I wanted god the hay-bound boy
before he ever knew the world
or saw my soul, all briar and want,
or wrecked his heart upon it.

Christmas Concert

—for Birdie Simmons

If the white keys are the beautiful seeming,
like the sun on clapboard, or bone clean beach,
and the black keys are gravity
gathered into itself, small dense ridges
that teach the white keys yearning,

harmony is the only handhold
my grandmother has left
as she pumps to sustain the chords—
The First Noel, We Three Kings.

She's playing for the church of herself.
The drapes of the sitting room are drawn,
the couch covered in plastic, preserved
for company who's to say won't come?

There's a dish where the candy has merged
all its sugars. If you lift one piece
the whole house starts to rise.

The silence between notes is where
she's headed. It grows every year,
though I learn this much later.

I think the black keys are memory,
and the white keys are sliding
like water over the pond's thin ice—
brave, blind, abandoned at birth,
except for the black keys.

Allegiance

I believe in the haloed snow in the streetlight
the weight of the dark lets down,
and the republic of the child's tongue
where the stars blink and die.
And the whole house full of father and mother
and the fogged windows
through which the lamps
seem kind, obedient creatures
burning the distance away. And the flag
of the boy who tears through the wind,
all scarf and shout, how nothing fills his bootprints
all the way to the brim,
how breath is a ripple on the dark
which is my country
when I am child enough again
and snow comes down like the kingdom of bread
breaking over the body for which it stands.

Hold on Me

The year I turned twelve I thought love
lived in the blond straw of the manger,
the naked face of the moon,
and AM rock and roll—

four-beat bass line, embellishing
waves of doo-wop, the brutal equation,
of say, the *Miracles* singing—

You treat me badly,
I love you madly,

which made sense to a Methodist,
for wasn't life an earthly penance
for the faithlessness of angels—
fallen apples of God's just eye?
And wasn't that Jesus, stapled
to the hilltop, his broken heart,
our valentine?

The year I was twelve, the stilted
grammar of greeting cards was love.
If you could just nail the rhyme scheme,
wouldn't human sympathy follow?

In other words, I knew nothing,
except crescendos and the closing
credits of movies felt like love,

and the way animals looked at you,
and that cut grass smelled
like what the word *unrequited*
would someday come to mean.

I lined my mother's lipsticks up
like so many beautiful bullets.
I'd never tasted a single kiss,
though I imagined one
hot as a wound.

...don't like you,
but I love you,

or some such anthem
crackled along the household air,
the year I was twelve.

Love was a brave little racket.

Through the back of the kitchen radio,
you could see it
in the glowing vacuum tube,
like a tiny bush that burned inside,
commanding the static to sing.

Trailer

—for J. Simmerman

The day is a dull gray blade.
Its left edge moves over the river
with a sound like wind in the cottonwoods.
The taste is metallic. An odor of fallen light
touches something in the heart
the way Trudy Baldwin's curves
touched the hearts of every sixth-grade boy
at Concord Elementary. Maybe not every boy,
and maybe it wasn't the heart, exactly,
she touched. But as I lay in bed listening low
to the Coasters, the Miracles, the *sha-las*
and *she-bops* of the background singers,
the beat was made of the way
Trudy walked, or just breathed.
When are you *not* too tired? I thought
I heard my father say
from the bedroom next to mine.
Every sound in the trailer traveled well.
The cheap bedsprings of my imagination
began to rattle among the low static
of the radio. There are nights you feel
so young you want to die. Want to skip
the dark moan of adulthood altogether,
sprout wings and wind upward
over the bedsprings and trailers
and Trudy Baldwins of the world.
Want to soar above the damply secret
serious business of earthbound bodies.
And you shall be a lamp unto your people.
And much shall come to pass, some voice
across the roof kept saying, or maybe
the holy curtains whispered me.
I knew that growing up was growing down.

I missed my wings already. *Adios. Boy voyage.*
The bedsprings were doing a kind of math
we hadn't gotten to in school. Though
some said Trudy had. Loose things
in the trailer—pennies, door knobs, hinges—
shook me all the way to sleep,
like when you throw a rock into the river
and the circles grow bigger and bigger,
then fainter, then finally the size
of the river itself.

II

Introduction to Philosophy

The professor had a hairless head
he polished like a monologue—

If you're robbed of your senses
of smell and taste and touch,
no eyesight or hearing...

He stepped to the window
and rapped a knuckle on the glass
representing the world.

Does it even exist?

This was Idealism, Bishop Berkeley.
This was 1968. Even I knew
the streets of major cities smoldered.
Martin Luther King's blood
on the balcony. Kennedy's
on the kitchen floor.

And if the predicate of a truth
is inherent in the subject,

say God exists
because look at the stars,
his mighty handiwork,

then are you not just saying,
I believe what I believe?

That was Kant on ontology.

If your average fell below a C
you got a letter, if you were male,

and a physical you tried your best
to fail, a buzzcut and a uniform,
and the nights
meant something different.

The distinction between *religion*
and *the religious*, according to Dewey,
was that the former was the latter
tricked out for power,
how the holy turns a profit.

I don't remember how I felt
about those high school friends
who couldn't make the grade,
or even buy the books. I held on,
underlining Kierkegaard's

deep down in the heart of piety
lurks mad caprice, which knows
it has produced its God.

The professor led us through the French,
kept walking to the window.
The names of the dead in the local news
were more and more familiar. I wasn't sure
there'd even *be* a country long.

There was a chapter on immortality
and one on semantic truth.
I studied enough to pass the course,
gained 3 credits, lost my faith.

We burned a village down for that,
this kid I knew told me later.

For No Man Would Say He Did a Favor to the Fountain by Drinking, or to the Light by Seeing

Or it was something like that
Saint Augustine said, having to do
with offering to God
what He already *was*—

more than enough water, ample
enough light to splash the moon
and the wave grabbing
at the wake of its brother.

God needed nothing, according to Augustine.
Whatever you gave, you gave to grow
toward that same need,
same nothing.

You stood on a pier, for instance,
and moonrise was too much to keep,
brittle wind in the lakeside trees.
Whatever you remembered
was too much, whatever
you'd forgotten,
since loss weighs more
than the lost thing itself.

It was early fall, though
the season was finer than that,
more precise, a season composed
of a single night, a single
thought. A souped up molecule
toted the moment
even deeper into the brain. Nobody
was watching the water
but you. Nobody saw

how wrong a saint could be,
saw God come down
begging on the lake,
call it moonlight frayed
like a fuse on the water,
call it pale as the color of kerosene.

You had your own problems
and projections, of course,
your own splintered heart to carry.
You could smell the other shore
like wet chalk on the wind.

But you saw it then
and you know it now.
Saint Augustine was wrong.
Whatever made this world
needs watching to live,
listening, swims all night
for what it lacks
even words to say.

Lines for the Cape Fear River

If I could give you anything
quicker and truer than the river
swims the sky down
to the size of the living,
I would. If I understood
the glazed look of water
on the move, or make, or mend,
I'd fend off cowardice
and tell you how it feels
to fall for a river,
or a woman, in a world
where sometimes the light
skims the surface for years
before it catches the gulls on fire
as they preen and flail
from the pilings of the far shore
where it's always paradise.

Elegy for the Sigh

Hardly anyone was sighing. There was,
in fact, a dearth of sighs,
the sigh going the way of the lute,
the bustle, the coat of mail.

Though many slept through turmoils
of love, and new fevers
swept through the spine at will,
shattering the lattices
of the ribcage,

hardly anyone suffered quietly
in the old style, schooled
in the art of sighing,

the way heroines in Bronte
could sigh, or poets
in English engravings, their soft
chins on their hands,
could sigh.

No one noticed the beloved
in things of little consequence.
For instance, the moon in daylight—
little broken wafer, waif-like,
waiting.

Hardly anyone waited,
like Jacob for Rachel—
six years, seven years,
like a stone in the field,
hardly anyone trusted time
that much.

Though whole neighborhoods gnashed
and wailed, wept
and even found love,

and the operatics of passion continued,
thumping against the walls of motels,

hardly anyone knelt for it,
crept for it, moored
himself to the longing required,

though love drove on, like a wheel
or a planet, no one,

hardly anyone, stood by a window
or a river, breathing the crucial vapors,
spending himself in sighs.

The Loon

The water winks open, the loon
is sewn onto the moonlit lake.
The lights of the far shore
could be anyone's necklace.
Wind rakes a little texture
across the surface. The loon
is the one live thing
on the lake, except the soul
which is debatable, and could
be the fading habitat of God,
or merely like this stain
the moon makes the water wear—
exquisite, migratory. *Dive*
you want to say,
but the loon is light as thread,
far away, and whatever you lack
cannot be wished under.

Apparition

That's the moon come down to drink,
that apparition on the water. Or
it's the milk of human kindness
slinking like an eel.

Wind tears the cottonwood away
leaf by handsized leaf.
Small waves slap the pilings.

What *is* the proper number of kisses
for a man to leave the world?
The average depth of melancholy?
The approximate wetness of hope?

It's very expensive tonight, the wind
in the lakeside trees. I don't see how
I could afford to listen

if not for you in the world,
as the leaves sail in their numbers,
somewhere deep, quick, and moonlike.

A Day on the Red Cedar River

The bass could hide forever in the way the water moves,
or the canoe glides past like a rip in the sunlight
that quickly mends itself, or the river does,
though there's a scar in the memory
by which the older fish survive.

We're *in* the river but not *of* the river
is what the crows keep preaching,
raucous bend after bend,
and the suspended shapes below us
and the snarl of currents
on the downside of sandbars,
and the floodtide trash
so high in the silver maples

we can't believe the same river
that carries us now, lightly
in the palm of the day, once
hurt its way through the trees,
gouged the high banks
back to raw geology, layers
of gravel and sandstone.

Today is another story. All bright things—
lacewings and damselflies, unbitten
lures wobbling back to the boat,
the splayed and strung out waters
that swing from the paddles,

belong to the stroke of noon,
which is long and musical
even to the tin ears
of those of us just passing through,

even though the fish aren't biting,
and the crows don't trust
how much better we feel
the more we cast for nothing.

And Who Shall Inherit

In corridors under the rain
the mole is a happy man.
The best part of grass is the bottom.
The best part of rain is the drumming
world where the earthworm rises
and the grub grows fat as a tulip
and the flimsy world of appearances
which so many make so much of
is a pleasant thrum, vague as heaven,
except for the seepage.

But the mole is a mudder.
His feet paddle forth, whiskers float out
to catch the trembling. The mole
is a mucker, following his nose
through the animate earth.
Grass weighs the rain.
The lawn's got the shivers.
Let the sun come and go
like any star. A happy man
is the mole, tucked in for the ride.

Day So Bright

Was-lost-but-now-I'm-found is the shade
of orange in the oaks today. *Was-frost
but-now-I'm-wind* is how they move.

It makes you want to plant an acorn
or something. Carve a gourd.
Trace the veins of a leaf out to the far
reaches of space. Fork some timothy.
Fescue?

It's a day so bright you can't help
but wish you were downright Amish,
like let's build a barn, quick and high,
haymaker swings of the hammers
like blue birdcalls over the stubbled fields.

Let there be pies, and brush-thick beards,
and bonnets over the politics.
Let the world blink like a stranded grain.
The day be sufficient. The feed-corn
rise to the brim of the crib.
The coal of sunset.

Let the heart be held still by the work of the day
retracing its route through the muscles,
and the night come down
like hair undone
in the star-like static of the cold.

On a Day Like This

—Thanksgiving: Rockford, Illinois

It's a springlike day at the brink
of November. Grass shines
an illusory green. Doves flail down
to the sunflower seeds and millet.
Not a door or a wing stays shut.
The golden squirrels of Rockford
are fat as housebound collies.
Pretty soon they'll need ladders
to climb onto the shingles
and bark out the code for joy.
What *is* winter but a ghost
of a chance? What is hunger
but a luxurious itch
soothed by the feeder's overflow,
the nailed up ears of corn, the plump
bitter acorns of the white oaks?
Some beast somewhere must know
better. Maybe *I* do. Maybe I don't.
I'd like for the grass to settle
this argument. I'd like this day
stained green in the mind for good—
no wind or night or need to remember.

It Gets to Me

The quarter moon is up and out
hours before the sun is down.
It's a small sail curved against the bright blue day.

But if the moon is a sail
what boat is this? My upturned face?
This boat of looking up and out?

It's been thirty years since people walked
on the moon, those long bounding strides
and the big ashy bootprints.

It's getting strange again, year
by year, a little less human,
a little more like never, or nearly
never touched at all.

I know the feeling. The moon at *night*
is the lovers' moon, the madman's moon,
the shapely moon of sonnets.

But this one, the daylit moon, carved
into the belly shape of a sail, but less
useful than a sail, if more precise,

seems as far away as love
when most of love is missing,
and the rest is barely moving,

and how much emptier the sky seems
when the moon's like this, out early,
is stranger than the moon to me.

There You Are

Strange how loss has a weight,
how a thing *subtracted*
bears down, bows the will.
Say a man walks from your door,
or life, or say it's a woman
because what is poetry
at a time like this
but the cadenced rerouting
of the personal? And
in that walking away
flows the shape of the door
and the road and the air
which is *nothing*, and yet
there you are, poetry
being what it is,
bowed by the burden
of a single self, a wholly
unprovable entity.

So what *is* the weight
you feel? Is it just
the theft of lightness?
Was the poet right who said
love is a buoyancy,
an amendment to gravity,
the weight of blood
and bone repealed?
So that only the loss of love
reveals the heart's true heft
and measure.

Or is it just the weight
of memory that oppresses,
like a door through which

she is always walking
in her dark shoes
and particular laughter?
There's a kind of fierceness
that reminds you
of driven snow. How sweet
a thing to brace against.

But isn't memory itself
invention, *airy nothing*,
as Shakespeare wrote? Or is
the context scrambled here?
Or was Shakespeare an invention,
just shaped from the shadow
of a man waving goodbye,
or say it's a woman,
poetry being what it is,
a way to speak a loss away,
plea for lightness,
impossible door.

The Deer

There's a herd of fallow deer on the hill
with springs for hooves and wariness
for a world around them; a single buck,
his antlers far too much for him—
top-heavy, necksore. The cost of attraction?
A tree sprouting from the forehead.

A little cattail swims in ditchwater.
Atop the milky silo, pigeons laze and putter.

It's light duty down on earth
some of the angels say,
though the old ones grin
with the pain of remembrance

as the buck lowers his lumbering head,
and the young deer scatter
just to watch him beg.

Tenderly

Some days it's best to stay put. Put forth
a feeler or two, at best, a wet finger to the wind,
but let's face it, some days

dash the hope you once harbored
bright as a boat, or high as a kite
above the dunes
where the wind was always willing.

The will flies off on its own some days,
and maybe it knows the back way home
or maybe it's no more loyal than a sparrow.

But once in a great gray bedridden while
the phone is better
off the hook, the smile is not
your umbrella, nor is the world

your oyster, nor a pearl to be found
among the grit and seawater.
Some days it's not determination

that sees you through, nor putting
the best foot forward, nor backward,
nor do you want *seen* through,
nor to lace them up at all.

Some days it's best to hunker down,
Dear, you say to yourself, tenderly.

The heart is a bunker some days,
a bathosphere, a bulb clenched deep
below the frost-line. Let it be.

Let bells ring the world awake, let birds
fly off into the freighted blue, let heaven
breed in the wildflower's face
for all you care. Some days are not for you.

Night Cicadas

Either something is gnawing its way
through a rivet, or the cicadas
have risen from their graves—
the thirteen and the seventeen
year cicadas, maybe the two
or three thousand year cicadas
for all I know, trembling
into song enough to scramble radar.
I feel it across my face and thought.
Life is short. Life is a day.
You can't accuse the cicadas
of not knowing their Leviticus,
their Isaiah. *And thou shalt*
hum like a dark heavenly wire.
And thou shalt cling
to the texture of tree bark.
Sing forth thy fellows
from stupor and darkness.
No wonder I can't sleep.
Over the okra beds
and bonnet-headed sunflowers,
over the limp frill of mimosa,
the cicadas ratchet up,
sustain, trail off,
then swell back to volume,
as if gathering the current
of all the slept years
only to let it go again,
unless this is my own mind
ground down to static, pulse
and wave and rasp of desire.

Where You Start

You have to admit sometimes the heart
is stationed there inside you, but far away.
I mean, you won't be visiting the heart
like a hill or a well or a windswept rock
the locals claim some dreamtime
God came down to tamper with.
It's living there, according to language,
splashes through you, in a sense,
drums you to sleep or love,
rows harder than your fear,
but far away. And the skin
is another county, the breast
a waning light. The muscles,
woven tighter than rain,
are a long day's ride
from where you start.
The ribs? an elegant barricade.
What you feel is map enough
is what you sometimes think.
But the heart is elsewhere
lodged inside. You won't
be visiting the heart.

Jet Lag

I pace the carpeted aisle of the air,
drink my cup of trembling juice, unlace
my shoes, eat light, forego the wine,
follow all the airline advice,

but still the heart lags miles behind
as I fly west from Shannon. The body
won't accept the gift of extra hours—
bonuses of daylight,

birds unroosted, stars put back
in their boxes. Though the *mind*
would steal time if it could—
longitudes flicking by like fenceposts,

years hoarded into great slippery piles;
the *body*—old shoe flung over the water,
lumpy Calvinist, is already preparing
to come down hard, mope and muddle for days.

I can feel it from here—being home,
but *not* home; being home, but not quite
being. I hold my cup. I pace the air.
I stand on the lawn gone haywire,

waiting for the unearned hours to pass,
waiting for the laggard heart—poor pilgrim,
dutiful pigeon, still lumbering
through the fogs over Newfoundland.

Looking Busy

Sure it's a ten-dollar watch
from the carousel at Walgreen's,
but if I lift my sleeve expensively,
crook my arm as if slightly fractured,
or spun of glass, or fractured glass,
then glance down

in the universal sign for
time is money,

how can even harsh winds
or hellfire keep me
from more than I can ever do?

All the merry note pads to attend.
Conversations to swim like glittery laps.
The daily mail to slice apart
and learn the meaning of.

Twelve numbers on this watch face,
months to the lunar year,
eggs to the dozen, disciples
of the Lord, though
they scattered like sparrows
when the hammering started,
didn't they? Wouldn't I?

Neither long for this world,
nor lost as I feel
is how I'm hoping to appear,
checking my watch,
as if the minutes themselves
depended on me,
like trains without conductors,
or bullets without vests.

My sleeve is pulled up.
My crooked arm in the air.
I'm trying to look late
or important at least.

The watch face rides
the blue ridge of a vein
like the moon on a vine
I'm much too busy
to let bother me.

A Night at St. Mary's

Codeine shears the fat black sheep.
One by one they leap over the tray
and still I can't find sleep.

Nurses rattle their needles about,
each one a rainy weather
I cast off into, my sail
as slim as old fashioned minutes,
the ones that used to go by.

Personally, I think
my prospects are leaking.
Personally, I think it's the dead
who won't give me rest.

They ring up and down the cold corridors
rustling their paper clothes.
The squeak of a shoe on linoleum
is the little black door the dead use.
Do they make a drug for that?

This bed is too much of a gurney
for sleep. I can feel the eagerness
in its twelve little wheels.

I watch the clock hands
struggle to move
through a medium thicker
than the plot of an opera.
It's no joke now. Thicker than fear.

Do they have a bell for that?
A button to push?

Do they have a nurse to hurry night
and me along,
make sleep my shepherd,
shut the door,
and blow the needles out?

Wash Your Face

Some mornings it's a harsh light
cast forth from the filaments
of the bathroom bulbs. They're so brainy,
bright, bald, the six of them over the mirror,
and I have to say some mornings
it's no flower, this face, no pretty
shell tossed up from the deeps
of dream, no sheen or starburst
to speak of. Nobody I know.
Not a face on a coin from a country
I've ever been to, not a face
you'd be able to spend and get very far
I'm afraid. Not a face you'd find
in a brand new wallet, a sample
friend or heart-throb, not even
a mug you'd finger for the beefy
detective, *that's the man*, you'd say,
but not of this face some mornings.
It's like all the parts never quite
come to, and how can a partial man
be guilty of anything but missing.
They don't seem pleased, the light bulbs.
You can tell what they're thinking
by the buzz and heat and shade
of yellow they've chosen for me.
It's nothing a tulip would wear,
or crocus, or even the common
jonquil. It's just wonder
worn thin, I guess. But when I look
some mornings there's less me
than I remember, and the light
seems to be cutting its losses,
and isn't helping anymore.

More and More Like Argon

I begin to take on the major characteristics
of the element *argon*—tasteless, colorless,

odorless, compassionless. Unable to combine, in fact,
with any other element. Let helium and neon

plead themselves blue in the face. Let flame
be applied. Let pressure.

The word *argon* in Greek means *idle,
not working.* I walk to the screen door

and sniff at the day. I notice the wind
is examining each leaf of the red oak,

both the dark and the light sides,
with a thoroughness that sounds

like falling water. More and more
I feel like the breath's worth of air

trapped inside the street lamp. The sun casts
a sheen over the oak leaves, nearly lifts

the glowing sides of the houses.
The air above town is agitated

into a blue-white arc. This is
as small as I can feel. Tiny birds

flutter and sail up in the popular gases—
oxygen, hydrogen, hunger and love.

This Tree

Somebody turn down the sky in the linden,
for the sky is blue and mean
and obscures the greater distances
where the universe whistles itself
through the deep reaches
and unmarked graves of starlight.

The sky's brightness on this winter day,
the way the blue fills in, coronates
and haloes the branches,
renders the linden a little ridiculous,
like a skeleton with a hairdo,
all teased out with no place to go
except through the wind's hands
over and over.

Why not let bones be bones
or what's a tree in winter for?
Why not turn down the light of sky
a notch, let the blue mind
its own gaudy business?

And let this tree, with its grip
of frozen ground, shake beauty loose
awhile, be stark and small
and free of wanting, whatever
wind moves through it like a will.

Linden in Winter

The linden is not so embraceable now
that the wind barrels down
from Alberta, swift
and fierce as God on his way
to some other portion of history,
someplace more Biblical maybe,
more in need of wrath, though
given the cold, the ripping snow,
maybe wrath is not the word,
but *will*, the sheer blind will of wind.
You can trace it across the weather map.
You can read it in the crazed dance
of the finch feeder, or the powder
swept from the garage roof
back up into the white sky.
The linden is stripped for the cold,
except for a few tough bracts,
a few blown about seeds.
The rest is down to the bone—
trunk, branch, and branch again—
stiff, skeletal, all the s words—
stoic, stern. It even sways a little,
though just enough to stand.
You could build a way of thinking,
or at least a train of thought
on how wind buckles the storm door,
drives the snow into drifts
against the diamonds
of the neighbors' chain link fence.
You could almost lean a life
on the emptiness that saves the tree,
how wind grazes the corridors
of what's not there,
and leaves the bones alive.

Snowy Landscape

—*"Reporters who defied the Russian ban on unauthorized
visits a few days ago encountered a snowy landscape—
picturesque if not for the desperation."*
Washington Post, *1/31/2000*

In the snow outside of Grozny
they were lining the bodies up
and the ones who weren't quite
bodies yet, with only
a missing limb or two,
but the breath still in them,

which is how you know
you're not a body, that
and the presence of pain
clenched into the face so tight
even the word *Allah*
had to struggle through the teeth
to gain the gates of heaven

as they lay in the snow
beside the overflowed hospital,
where the surgeon who wasn't
remotely a surgeon
amputated by flashlight,
the bad news being—no syringes,
the good news—no medicine
anyway

unless the snow itself
was a kind of medicine
as it covered the hills,
wheelruts and hedges,
granting the ruins
of the distant treeline

a sense of lightness,

except for the quickening blast,
the deep percussive thud
like some larger heart-
beat under the snow
enveloping their own.

Snow on the lips
a time or two.
Snow on the empty sleeve.

Snow like morphine
might have felt
whitened the rooftops into wings
about to fold or unfold
as I looked out on Emery Street
in the middle of the Wisconsin winter,

the light moving over the drifted lawn
like watching a dream
cross the face of a sleeper,
and you know something's happening,
but you don't know how deep,
since you're not the sleeper.
You're just watching from the window,
looking out at the ordinary snow.

Questions About the Linden

Should the linden consider itself
more of a boxwood or candelabra?
More a way station for the winter
juncos, or map of the light
of the last forty summers?
I think of the body's trees—
prophetic tree of bones,
rowdy tree of blood
with its one red root,
tree of the nerves
that leaf into the impulse
to fathom, even fear
the trees of blood and bone.
Should the linden be more
a mirror of that? Or left alone
to dwell on its own quiet god
whose blessing is absence,
whose will is unknown,
whose angels are wrecked
in the silhouettes of branches
forbidden to believe or forget?

III

What About the Light on the Window?

I mean the bounced back light
that mirrors my own face
looking in, my body cast
on the dark outside
of the hotel window
like something not quite
developed, a man still
in the midst of transmission.
There are spaces, places you
can see through my body
to the parked cars
and pillars of the downtown
cloverleaf—what a beautiful word
for everyone hurrying, for the tangle
of traffic that travels my shoulders
and chest. What a shame
for the light to stream so far
and be stricken on a hotel
window in Albany, New York,
and me in the spell of my own
vain moment, as if I contained
what hurried behind me
and where they were going
and even the mechanical surf
sound of car wheels on concrete.
And even the skyline—spire,
wedge, thicket of aerials.
What a vague shape a body
makes when you're looking in,
barely more than a window
itself. What a slim thing
for the light to bounce back,
having washed so far

in little packets and waves.
I could look a long time
at the steadiness
of parked cars, the flourish
of blown paper that proves
the wind, the traffic navigating
the cloverleaf in my shoulder,
through my shoulder, the skyline
of Albany like a city inside,
but not *really* inside, whatever
light grants as it goes.

What About the Lilacs?

They grow big as houses here, the lilacs do.
I'll bet a man could live in one, throw
weddings among the cordate leaves
if people fell in love enough.

Blossoms the size of pets or furniture,
roots sunk deep as Baptist hymns,
although it's mostly Lutherans here
because of the sandy soil, or Catholics
lured by the false cathedrals
light pencils down
through the pines,

and one tiny temple, with
hollyhocks up to the windows
and paint flecking away
from the points of the star.

They spring up everywhere, the lilacs,
like weeds, or doubt, or alibis.

Why does the heavy scent of the flowers
always remind me *backwards* though,
to some enormous room of a time
I don't think I even lived in?

They smell like twilight waiting to happen.
No, they smell like the desire
to belong to another kingdom:
no words, no human borders there.

But all the best shrubs are fiction,
aren't they? The bees race in and out.
The sky shoots a vague blue glance.

If I walked out this minute

and breathed open
a balloon-sized blossom,

wouldn't my breath steal *me* away
and into the general life of things,
the backlog of cool disorder

when I was a brave and well-loved boy,
or woman, or wind, and lilac
my native tongue?

An Exercise in Waking Up on Davenport Street

A particle of sun glances over
the drooping zinnias. A waffling

of tires over the asphalt
leaves me with an emptiness

twice the size of the room,
a scientific anomaly

native to these parts. It's like
snagging a huge, dark fish

on the tiny hook-end of a word.
So how can I hold such a wise,

imaginary creature? I feel the air
leaking out of the enterprise already.

A few minutes later I notice
the sun is having a heyday,

and that's all it takes. I feel
somewhat lovely and ashamed.

One after another the doors
in the flowers open.

One after another the dewdrops
spring from the grass blades

more or less into my arms.

Self-Improvement

It might as well be some port of the moon
for all the likelihood and proximity,
and yet I'm trying again, embarking
you might say, upon a new self,

a self more unflinching, firm of will,
a virtual boulder of a guy.

Does a *dog* wake up and yearn
to be a better man?
Does a leaf? An October wind
wish itself more visible? Less volatile?

Outside, the oak leaves wince
and fall, but never seemed
more like themselves than now—
a dropped puzzle of identical pieces
the rain won't solve, the whole
winter won't.

I'd like to be a Buddhist,
that's it—give up the self altogether,
or nail it, deed by deed,
to the comely absolute.

It's just the part about *life is pain*,
that holds me back.

Or maybe a foot-washing Baptist
like my great-grandfather,
George Washington Rust,
with his broom-stiff beard
and buffalo nickels,

a man redeemed way past
the ruckus of *I want,*
and *Will she ever?*

and *What happens if?*

It's like having a committee of damp matches
for a brain, this flimsiness of self,
every thought amended
just at the brink of flame.

Which is why I'm setting out again,
repenting my passports, fingerprints,
though it might as well be
a speck among stars, this rock-hard
saved and glistening self I'm after.

Mirth

And so I set out
and instead of a life
was the going out to find one

and instead of the one
were the several to choose from—

the baby boy swaddled in mirth,
as I remember,

the knot-headed ingrate
who romped through the book of religion
in search of the angel
who sowed the most doubt,
the wake of whose wingbeat
felt most like a fever,

the bruised lover
who need not be mentioned
further,

the *attempting-to-age-
with-some-degree-of-grace*
and I don't mean in the Pauline
sense of the word,
but simply looking good,

and instead of the choosing
the days blinked down
of their own sweet accord

and instead of remembering
the mirth seemed more or less
molded from the distance
between childhood and now

as if nothing ever happened
until I looked back,
neither starlight nor fever
nor life I set out to find.

You Miss It

It's less lonely than it used to be,
what with the forests stripped down
to the minimum now, and the white lines
painted on the Oakwood Mall lot

and the cars parked like brothers,
in order of their arrival,
the sheen of the Lord upon them,
however, the last as blessed
with brightness as the first.

It's less lonely without the animals
broadcasting their strange sense
of themselves, as if being were enough,
if you sang it incessantly
from a high enough branch,
or possibly barked it into the night.

It's less lonely without the barking,
or the baying, or the night itself,
the small eyes clicking off and on
from the brambles, the lit green eyes,
the yellow. Though you miss it,
the loneliness, the size of it mostly,

the way you rose up to meet it
in fear, and were enlarged,
somehow, by the rising
and your own fumbling for sounds,
sequences, syllables

to cast yourself like a spell
into the midst of something
you neither made, nor imagined,
nor could keep from imagining.

Last Day

The last day of the world is in the ash tree.
It may or may not come down. The large upward
branches move like the ache of any rooted thing.
The smaller branches seem to shiver, the leaves
turned inside out. They're cold as minnows, high
as their shadows will let them go.

You might say it's just the wind of this September day
that stirs and riffles the leaves. Or maybe
some inward sighing from the long history of ashes—
the generations standing in rows, knock
of the ax, lick of the fire, the slow whitening
and the winters locking down the green doors
of the will.

But it looks like the last day of the world,
the way the branches flex and buckle,
and the leaves fill the air with the long hush
that comes after whatever we thought
we'd be thinking about forever.

Scene from a Window near the Austin Airport

What I never expected was the knottiness
of things, how the wind gets tangled
in the rows of trees, *cedar elms*, I think,
and they won't let go, or the wind won't,
a commotion that sounds like running
water over rock a quarter-mile away.
And something reaches in the brain
for a place like that, an actual river—
the Upper Black in Missouri, or
the lower reaches of the Chippewa
as it sweeps the sandstone down to grit,
as if that might untangle the knot
or make it fast enough to hold.
I'm trying to distinguish between the two
when a southbound jet rumbles over
so low the vibration inhabits the house.
A wave runs through the wall studs,
woodwork, shakes the nailheads
blind as constellations in daylight.
The window glass quivers, or maybe
the world, because what you *see*
you *get,* at least at gut level,
at least as long as the quivering lasts.
And it's only as the rumble diminishes,
the glass goes still, that I realize
I never heard the wind inside this house,
but made it up from the motion,
the black-green swirl of branches,
the lifetime of other trees I've heard
the wind move through like a river,
which is what I mean about the knottiness
of things, as if the brain doesn't care
about getting it right, but just
wants to hear the water.

Lullaby

The little white day rode out on the water.
Many forces were aligned.

Waves tall as steeples, ships
with anger in their holds.

The odds were against any given thing,
yet the sea was busy as a cauldron of bees—

white day, black day, all manner
of dolphin and sublunar motion.

The little white day bobbed like a melody.
A friendly, slightly drunken one.

Various hopes were pinned to the mast.
We were among them, I think, you and I,

though this all happened in another tongue,
written and erased morning and night

almost forever in the backhand of surf,
the vowels all broken into sand by now,

the consonants, if you can call them that,
wet and mishappen as the lowliest mollusk.

The little white day more like something
you'd try to sell a child at night,

when running out of what to sing,
and sleepy yourself from all the rocking.

Shoreline Ecology

Because there's never enough to go around
the afternoon wind in the cottonwoods
along the south shore of Erie

borrows the sound of June rain
through the catalpa leaves of western Kentucky,
circa 1962, combined

with the sound of small sticks
starting to burn
when you'd almost given up on the fire.

And the stutter of planes rising from Toledo
above the scattered clouds
is the quirky drum of the stethoscoped heart
of a man who spent his whole life
listening to reason,

yet the other world is there
in the backbeat, the bent
part of the rhythm.

The waves, of course, are what you wanted
and had, and can't get back
or let go, until the wind picks up.

Then the whitecaps and backspills
are the collective hushings
of all the children who couldn't sleep
for fear of what they'd never say,
and all the hushings to come.

And the clam shells mimic the hollow of harbors
and tightly cupped hands,
because there's never enough,

and a little gets through.

And the gulls have taken the best note
of my anger, and multiplied it
over the mouth of the estuary

where the water moves all ways at once,

and the minnows are hiding
disguised as their shadows, in glitter
and number, though never enough.

Goldfinches

You might say the sky is a kiss,
but where would that get you
this early in the morning?

You might walk out under an arc
so blue it almost erases the mind.

What isn't erased is whatever
has been moving through the mint—
the odor of that, and the sweet rot
of tomatoes too far down the vine,

and a season's worth of small things
starting to soften into their deaths.
Think of the sheer number of wings
it takes to generate a summer,

how they all go down into the grass,
all the veined iridescence
that held aloft the hum
and whine of wanting to pass it on.

The sky is as blue as the wake of that.

Goodbye is the kind of kiss
the sky might be. Kiss of the light
winging off into the blind reaches
beyond anything but belief.

Acrid kiss that instigates the blood
as you watch the finches robbing
the small branches of the sunflowers.

They ride the wet stems like waves,
wire-walkers, bright rodeos
among the flowerbeds. Kiss of whose
hunger lets them be that light.

This Cup

It's one of those white ceramic cups
from the dawn of American diners,
tall as a big man's hand is wide.

A mug, really, which is also the word
for the roadworn face of the man
or the face of the man
the big hand once pummeled,
though not for meanness sake.

It's the cup of necessity, brutally
unadorned, thick as the haze
the sun struggles through
on its way to the work week.

The kind of cup a woman pours
in a booth just off I-80, a cup
you'd have to go some to break,

maybe drive all night from Kearney
to Coralville, kidneys ringing
from the played-out struts
and the diesel's vibrations.

Too tired to call what's left of home,
you'd have to nod and slide
down the Naugahyde seat,
elbowing the cup into air,

but even then it might not shatter,
the force of the fall muted
by the thickness and slight flare
of the mouth, and something else
the cup found out in the fires of the kiln

about the strength of emptiness.

It's a cup for remembering the size
of a life, your own muddled reflection
through the streamers of steam
you whisper away, or stir and diminish.

It's the cup of uprightness after awhile,
the very way an object ought to feel
on earth—awake, a weight

you can lift and lean into,
that stiffens the wrist and resolve—

cup enough to build a morning around
once the nerves begin to fire, the mind
unfolding like a map,

the day unfolding around the fact,
a shape so blunt and true, this cup
you can't put down.

Recent Cleveland State University
Poetry Center Prize Winning Titles:

Winner CSU Poetry Center Prize, 2000
The Largest Possible Life by Alison Luterman
CSU Poetry Series LIX, ISBN 1-880834-52-9
(paper) 112 pp., $14.00.

Winner CSU Poetry Center Prize, 2001
Before the Blue Hour by Deirdre O'Connor
CSU Poetry Series LX, ISBN 1-880834-55-3
(paper) 80 pp., $14.00.

Winner CSU Poetry Center First Book Competition, 2002
The Saint of Letting Small Fish Go by Eliot Khalil Wilson
CSU Poetry Series LXI, ISBN 1-880834-58-8
(paper) 88 pp., $14.00.

Winner CSU Poetry Center Open Competition, 2002
Double Exposure by Sarah Kennedy
CSU Poetry Series LXII, ISBN 1-880834-59-6
(paper) 88 pp., $14.00.

Winner CSU Poetry Center First Book Competition, 2003
Guide to Native Beasts by Mary Quade
CSU Poetry Series LXIII, ISBN 1-880834-61-8
(paper), 96 pp., $14.00.

Winner CSU Poetry Center Open Competition, 2003
The Job of Being Everybody by Douglas Goetsch
CSU Poetry Series LXIV, ISBN 1-880834-62-6
(paper), 72 pp., $14.00.

Winner CSU Poetry Center First Book Competition, 2005
The Small Mystery of Lapses by Christopher Burawa
CSU Poetry Series LXV, ISBN 1-880834-68-5
(paper) 96 pp., $14.00.

Winner CSU Poetry Center Open Competition, 2005
Hunger Wide as Heaven by Max Garland
CSU Poetry Series LXVI, ISBN 1-880834-69-3
(paper) 104 pp., $14.00.

The Cleveland State University Poetry Center is the publisher of over 150 collections of contemporary poetry since 1971.

To place a book order, call 1-888-278-6473 toll free (216-687-3986 locally). Fax: 216-687-6943.
E-mail: poetrycenter@csuohio.edu.
Website: www.csuohio.edu/poetrycenter.
Titles also available on amazon.com.

Cleveland State University Poetry Center
Department of English
2121 Euclid Avenue
Cleveland OH 44115-2214